Money Mastery

Unlocking the Secrets to Financial Freedom

A Mini Guide for Learning the
Art of Financial Independence,
Investment, and Wealth
Creation

Mason Griffin

Money Mastery
Unlocking the Secrets to Financial Freedom

A Mini Guide for Learning the Art of Financial
Independence, Investment, and Wealth Creation

Mason Griffin

Table Of Contents

Introduction

- The Importance of Money Management
- Understanding Your Relationship with Money

Part 1: Building a Strong Financial Foundation

Part 2: Saving and Investing for the Future

Part 3: Building Wealth and Achieving Financial Freedom

- **Chapter 7:** Creating Passive Income Streams
- **Chapter 8:** Real Estate Investing
- **Chapter 9:** Starting and Growing a Business

Part 4: Maintaining Financial Success

- **Chapter 10:** Protecting Your Wealth with Insurance
- **Chapter 11:** Estate Planning and Legacy Building
- **Chapter 12:** Staying on Track and Adjusting Your Strategy

Conclusion

- The Power of Money Mastery
- Taking Action to Achieve Financial Freedom

INTRODUCTION

Our decisions are influenced by money, which is an important component of our life. Our financial situation has a big impact on how happy we are, whether we are intending to buy a house, establish a business, or retire. However, a lot of people have trouble managing their money wisely and as a result, they lose out on chances to accumulate wealth and achieve financial freedom.

This is where "Money Mastery: Unlocking the Secrets to Financial Freedom" comes in. We will look at useful tactics and tried-and-true methods in this book to assist you in taking charge of your money and building a prosperous and secure life. We'll go into issues like setting a budget, controlling debt, saving money and investing it, generating passive income, investing in real estate, launching a business, and much more.

This book is for you whether you are just beginning your financial path or want to advance your wealth-building. You can alter your relationship with money, attain financial freedom, and lead the life you really want by learning the secrets of money mastery. Let's therefore begin this fascinating trip to financial prosperity!

PART ONE:

Building a Strong Financial Foundation

Building a solid financial foundation is the first step toward financial freedom. This entails clearly defining your financial objectives, developing a budget, and handling your debt. Each of these topics will be thoroughly covered in this section, along with helpful advice on how to establish a strong financial foundation.

Chapter 1:

Setting Financial Goals

Building a solid financial foundation starts with setting financial goals. It is vital to have a distinct understanding of your goals and the procedures necessary to achieve them. This chapter will discuss the significance of creating financial goals and offer you helpful advice on how to do so.

Why Setting Financial Goals is Important

Setting financial goals is critical because it helps you:

1. **Define Your Priorities:** Setting financial objectives enables you to focus on what's essential to you and prioritize your expenditure. You can make sure your money is being spent on the things that mean most to you by determining your priorities.

2. **Stay Motivated:** A thorough understanding of your goals will help you stay motivated. Setting financial goals gives one a sense of direction and purpose, which makes it simpler to stay on task and avoid detours.

3. **Measure Your Progress:** You can track your development and progress by setting financial goals. It assists you in keeping track of your successes and pinpointing your areas for development.

4. **Make Better Financial Decisions:** You may make wiser financial decisions by setting financial goals. You may make selections that forward your goals when you are fully aware of what you're aiming towards.

Tips for Setting Financial Goals

1. Define Your Goals: Defining your objectives while making financial goals is the first step. Consider your immediate and long-term goals first. Long-term objectives could be saving for retirement or purchasing a home, while short-term objectives could be paying off debt or creating an emergency fund.

2. Make Your Goals Specific: Your financial objectives should be precise and measurable. Instead of stating that you want to "save more money," for instance, give yourself a particular target, such as "saving $500 per month for the next 12 months." Your objectives become more attainable and manageable as a result.

3. Set Realistic Goals: Big objectives are excellent, but it's also crucial to create achievable, realistic goals. Setting unattainable goals can cause you to become frustrated and ultimately give up on your financial aspirations. When establishing your goals, take into account your income, expenses, and overall financial condition.

4. Write Down Your Goals: Setting down your goals in writing can keep you motivated and focused. It serves as a tangible reminder of your goals and might support your continued progress.

5. Review Your Goals Regularly: Regularly review your financial objectives to make sure you're on the right path. If you're having trouble moving forward, change your plan of action to begin moving again. Regular reviews also provide you the chance to acknowledge your successes and revise your objectives when your financial condition changes.

6. Make Your Goals Challenging: Setting reasonable objectives is crucial, but you should also push yourself. Too simple of a goal may not be enough of a motivator. Think about establishing challenging objectives that will take you beyond your comfort zone.

7. Break Your Goals Down into Smaller Steps: Your goals may become simpler to accomplish if you divide them into smaller, more manageable tasks. If your objective is to save $10,000 for a down payment on a home, for instance, divide that amount into more manageable monthly savings targets.

Set attainable financial goals using the advice in this chapter to get started on the path to a more stable financial future.

Examples of Financial Goals

Here are some examples of financial goals that you can set for yourself:

1. Emergency Fund: Having an emergency reserve is a crucial financial objective. Try to put three to six months' worth of spending aside in a savings account that is simple to get to.

2. Debt Reduction: Another typical financial objective is to pay off high-interest debt, such as credit card debt, personal loans, or student loans. Establish a deadline for paying off your debt and monitor your progress as you go.

3. Retirement Savings: A long-term financial objective that necessitates persistent work is saving for retirement. Establish a target for how much you want to contribute annually to your retirement account and figure out how much you need to save for retirement.

4. Home Ownership: For many people, purchasing a home represents a substantial financial objective. Determine the down payment amount you require, then begin saving for it. To be eligible for a better mortgage rate, you might also want to set a target for raising your credit score.

5. Education: You can increase your income in the future by investing in your education. Establish a target for the amount of money you wish to put aside for student loans or for advancing your education.

Strategies for Achieving Your Financial Goals

After deciding on your financial objectives, you must create a strategy to reach them. The following tactics can assist you in reaching your financial objectives:

1. Create a Budget: An effective tool for money management is a budget. You can use it to find places where you can cut costs and save money to use toward your financial objectives.

2. Automate Your Savings: Saving consistently is made simpler by automating your savings. To make sure you are contributing to your objectives each month, set up automated payments to your savings account.

3. Track Your Progress: You can stay motivated by tracking your development toward your financial objectives on a regular basis. To track your progress and make necessary adjustments to your plan, use a spreadsheet or budgeting tool.

4. Find Ways to Increase Your Income: Your financial objectives may be accomplished more quickly if your income increases. Find ways to increase your income, such as by taking on a side business or requesting a raise at work.

5. Stay Accountable: Share your financial objectives with a responsible party. This might be a friend, relative, or financial expert. Having a somebody to update on your progress helps keep you motivated and on course.

To lay a solid financial basis, financial goals must be established. It supports your ability to set spending priorities, maintain motivation, and make wiser financial choices. You can create realistic financial goals and strive toward a more secure financial future by implementing the advice and techniques provided in this chapter.

Chapter 2:

Creating A Budget

Creating a Budget That Works for You

A budget is an essential tool for good money management. It enables you to develop financial objectives, comprehend your cash inflows and outflows, and make wise spending choices. We will examine how to develop a budget that works for you in this chapter.

Step 1: Determine Your Income

To start a budget, you must first ascertain your income. This includes any earnings from your employment, financial investments, or side businesses. Make a note of your monthly income total after calculating it.

Step 2: Track Your Expenses

Keeping track of your expenses is the next stage. Identifying all of your monthly spending on bills, groceries, entertainment, and other expenses is required. To keep track of your spending, you can use a spreadsheet, a budgeting app, or a pen and paper.

Step 3: Categorize Your Expenses

It's time to categorize your expenses after you've listed every one of them. Housing, transportation, food, entertainment, utilities, and debt repayment are examples of common expense categories. You can find areas where you can reduce your expenditure by categorizing your expenses.

Step 4: Determine Your Monthly Expenses

Your total monthly expenses can be calculated by adding together all of your spending for each category. You'll be able to see where your money is going each month as a result.

Step 5: Compare Income and Expenses

It's time to compare your earnings and outgoings. You're in good shape if your revenue exceeds your outgoings. You will need to change your spending, though, if your income is lower than your costs.

Step 6: Make Adjustments

You will need to change your spending habits if your expenses are more than your income. Find areas where you can reduce spending. By meal planning and taking advantage of bargains, for instance, you might be able to lower your food price. As an alternative, you might need to search for methods of raising your income, such starting a side business or asking for a pay boost at work.

Step 7: Set Goals

Setting financial objectives is the final step in creating a budget. Your objectives ought to be specific, measurable, and doable. You could, for instance, set a goal of paying off your credit card debt in the next year. You can stay motivated and focused on your financial goals by setting clear goals.

Additional tips for creating a successful budget

1. Be Practical: Be practical when estimating your income and expenses for your budget. Never under or overestimate your income or spending.

2. Track Your Spending: You can find areas where you can reduce your spending by tracking your spending on a regular basis.

3. Use Budgeting Tools: Effective money management is possible because to the many budgeting tools and apps that are already available.

4. Make Adjustments as Needed: You should be able to make changes to your budget as your income and expenses change.

5. Celebrate Your Success: Celebrate your financial victories as you go. Take the time to celebrate your accomplishments and maintain your motivation, whether you're paying off debt or hitting a savings target.

Examples of Budgeting Methods

To manage your funds, you can utilize a variety of budgeting techniques. Here are a few well-known examples:

1. 50/30/20 Budgeting Rule: According to this budgeting principle, you should set aside 20% of your salary for savings and debt repayment and 50% of your income for needs (such housing, food, and transportation), 30% for discretionary spending, and 10% for entertainment and hobbies.

2. Zero-Based Budgeting: With this approach of budgeting, every dollar of your income is allotted to a particular spending or savings target. This implies that the difference between your income and expenses should be zero.

3. Envelope System: Cash is allocated for each spending category in individual envelopes using this method of budgeting. You can keep inside your budget by just being able to spend what is in each envelope for that area.

4. Reverse Budgeting: With this approach, you save money before paying for your expenses. You set aside a specified portion of your salary for savings, and you divide the remainder among your expenses.

5. 80/20 Budgeting Rule: According to this budgeting principle, you should set aside 20% for savings and debt reduction and 80% of your income for expenses.

Pick the way of budgeting that best suits your needs and your financial condition. Never be reluctant to experiment with different approaches until you find one that works for you.

The first step toward achieving financial stability and freedom is to create a budget. You may make a budget that works for you by figuring out your income, keeping track of your expenses, classifying your spending, comparing your income and expenses, making adjustments, and defining financial goals. Keep in mind to be reasonable, monitor your expenditure, use budgeting tools, adjust as necessary, and recognize your accomplishments along the way. You can take charge of your money and reach your financial objectives by implementing a budgeting strategy that works for you.

Chapter 3:

Managing Debt and Improving Credit Score

Debt is a widespread financial problem that many people face. It may stress you out, make you anxious, and hinder your efforts to obtain financial security and freedom. We'll talk about managing your debt, getting rid of it, and raising your credit score in this chapter.

Understanding Debt

Debt is sums of money due to creditors or lenders. Debt can take many different forms, including credit card debt, personal loans, school loans, car loans, and mortgages. When you borrow money, you consent to pay it back over time with interest. Your credit score may suffer if you don't pay your debts on time, and this could put you in financial trouble.

Managing Debt

Understanding your debt responsibilities, including the amount you owe, interest rates, and payment due dates, is crucial for effective debt management. These actions will help you manage your debt;

1. **Establish a Debt Repayment Plan:** To organize and pay off your debt, you can utilize the debt snowball or avalanche approach. The debt snowball strategy calls for making minimum payments on all debts while paying off the smallest balance first. You start with the smallest loan and work your way up until you have paid off every debt. The debt avalanche strategy calls for making minimum payments on all other debts while paying off the obligation with the highest interest rate first.

2. **Make prompt payments:** Late payments can lower your credit score and result in fees and penalties that raise your debt. To guarantee on-time payments, set up automatic payments or reminders.

3. **Negotiate Interest Rates:** By negotiating lower interest rates with your creditors or lenders, you can eventually pay less in interest.

4. Think about debt consolidation: Debt consolidation entails consolidating various loans with high interest rates into one with a reduced interest rate. This may ease debt management and lower your monthly payments.

How to Boost Your Credit Score

Your credit score, which consists of three digits, is a reflection of your creditworthiness and capacity for debt repayment. You can obtain credit, get loans with reduced interest rates, and improve your credit score. The following advice will help you raise your credit score:

1. Pay your bills on time: Your credit score is mostly influenced by your payment history. Make sure to pay all of your bills on time, including credit card, loan, and utility obligations.

2. Keep Your Credit Utilization Ratio Low: The credit utilization ratio measures how much of your available credit you are really using. To keep your credit score high, try to keep this percentage under 30%.

3. Monitor Your Credit Report: To find errors, disputes, or unauthorized activity that could lower your credit score, review your credit report frequently.

4. Avoid Closing Credit Accounts: Your available credit may be decreased and your credit utilization may rise as a result of closing credit accounts.

Additional Debt Management Techniques;

There are further methods you can employ in addition to the ones described in the preceding section to effectively manage your debt.

1. Consider Debt Settlement: Debt settlement is a method of negotiating with creditors or debt collectors to lower the amount of debt owing. In order to settle the debt for less than what is owed, this approach entails making a lump-sum payment or consenting to a payment schedule.

2. Seek Professional Help: Consult a financial expert, debt counselor, or credit counselor if you need help managing your debt. These experts can offer advice on how to establish a debt repayment strategy, bargain with creditors, and efficiently manage your finances.

3. Refinance High-Interest Debt: Refinancing is the process of replacing an existing loan with a new one that has a lower interest rate. This can lower your monthly payments and help you save money on interest payments.

4. Reduce Expenses: Examine your spending to find places where you might make savings. Take into account lowering your discretionary spending on things like entertainment, subscriptions, and eating out.

5. Use Different Types of Credit: Having a variety of credit available to you, including loans, credit cards, and mortgages, can raise your credit score. This demonstrates to lenders your ability to responsibly manage various forms of credit.

6. Limit the Number of Credit Accounts You Open: Your credit score may suffer if you open several credit accounts quickly. It's ideal to progressively open fresh accounts over time.

7. Maintain a Long Credit History: Your credit score is influenced by the length of your credit history. To keep a long credit history, avoid canceling your oldest credit accounts.

8. Regularly check your credit score: Regularly checking your credit score will help you spot areas that need improvement and keep track of any alterations to your credit report.

Debt management and credit score improvement involve self-control, dedication, and perseverance. You may take charge of your finances, attain financial stability, and gain financial freedom by utilizing the techniques described in this chapter. Keep track of your progress, stay organized, and ask for help if you need it. You may reach your financial objectives and learn the keys to financial freedom with some time and effort.

Part Two:

Saving and Investing for the Future

One of the most crucial financial habits you can form is saving and investing for the future. It is crucial for accomplishing your long-term financial objectives, including as purchasing a home, retiring comfortably, or financing the education of your children. This section will examine the advantages of saving and investing and offer helpful pointers to get you started.

Why Saving and Investing is Important

There are several advantages to saving and investing for the future, including:

1. **Increasing Wealth:** You can accumulate wealth over time if you continuously invest and save. The power of compounding allows even modest contributions to rise dramatically over time.

2. **Achieving Long-Term Goals:** Your long-term financial objectives, such as as purchasing a

home, retiring comfortably, or funding your children's education, can be attained with the aid of saving and investing.

3. Giving monetary security: A financial safety net can be created through investing and saving in the event of unplanned expenses, such as sudden medical costs or job loss.

4. Generating Passive Income: Investing in assets like stocks, bonds, or real estate can produce passive income that can be used as a complement to your regular income and as retirement security.

Some Tips for Saving and Investing

1. Start Early: The more time your money has to develop, the earlier you should start investing and saving. Regularly made tiny payments, however, can add up over time.

2. Make Specific Goals: Establish specific financial objectives, such as saving for retirement or a down payment on a home. You'll be able to focus and stay motivated using this.

3. Create a Budget: You can find opportunities to cut costs and free up money for savings and investments by making a budget.

4. Make a variety of investments: Your potential earnings can improve and risk can be reduced by diversifying your investments. Take into account purchasing a variety of stocks, bonds, and other assets.

5. Spend money on tax-advantaged accounts: Tax-advantaged accounts, like 401(k)s, IRAs, and 529 plans, can offer substantial tax advantages and encourage you to put more money down for the future.

6. Be Patient: Investments are a long-term tactic. Remain focused on your long-term objectives and refrain from acting rashly in response to short-term market volatility.

Conclusion

A crucial financial habit that can help you reach your long-term objectives and ensure financial security is saving and investing for the future. You can build wealth and achieve financial freedom by getting started early, setting specific goals, developing a budget, diversifying your investments, and making investments in tax-advantaged accounts. Keep in mind to be patient, keep your eyes on the prize, and, if necessary, seek out expert guidance. You can safeguard your financial future and reap the rewards of years of wise saving and investing with a little time and effort.

Chapter 4:

Saving for Emergencies and Short-Term Goals

Saving money for short-term objectives and emergencies is a crucial component of financial planning. Saving for short-term goals can help you reach significant milestones, such as a trip or a down payment on a home, while having an emergency fund can serve as a safety net for unforeseen circumstances, like a job loss or a medical emergency. This chapter will discuss the value of setting aside money for short-term objectives and emergencies as well as offer advice on how to manage your savings well.

The Importance of Saving for Emergencies

A savings account set aside expressly for unforeseen costs, such a medical emergency or auto repair, is known as an emergency fund. Having an emergency fund can assist you in avoiding debt that can harm your finances, such as high-interest credit card debt. Here are some justifications on why it's crucial to have emergency funds:

1. Peace of Mind: Knowing that you have a safety net in case of unforeseen circumstances might be a comfort when you have an emergency fund.

2. Avoiding Debt: You may stay away from debt that can harm your finances, such as high-interest credit card debt, by using an emergency fund.

3. Investment opportunities: When your emergency fund is fully financed, you might have the chance to invest the remaining money, which can help you accumulate wealth over time.

1. Determine Your Target: As a general rule, you should have three to six months' worth of living expenses set aside in your emergency fund. However, this sum may change based on your unique situation.

2. Start Automatic Savings: You may constantly add to your emergency fund without having to think about it by setting up automatic savings.

3. A High-Yield Savings Account may be an option: Through greater interest rates, a high-yield savings account can speed up the growth of your emergency fund.

4. Increase Savings with Windfalls: Gains, like tax refunds or bonuses, can be used to increase your emergency fund and hasten the completion of your savings goals.

Saving for Short-Term Goals

Saving for immediate objectives, like a trip or a down payment on a house, can help you reach significant milestones and serve as inspiration for ongoing financial planning. Here are some justifications for the significance of short-term goal saving:

1. Achieving Milestones: Short-term goals, like a dream vacation or a down payment on a home, might help you reach significant milestones.

2. Building Financial Habits: You may learn sound financial practices like budgeting and living within your means by saving for short-term goals.

3. Motivation for Long-Term Goals: Realizing short-term objectives might inspire you to continue financial planning and keep you focused on your long-term objectives.

Additional Tips for Saving for Short-Term Goals

1. Specific Goal setting: A clear savings target helps keep you motivated and concentrated on accomplishing your objective.

2. Have Savings Plan: You can break down your goal into doable chunks and monitor your progress over time by making a savings plan.

3. Cut Back on Expenses: You may have more money to put toward your savings goals if you reduce your spending.

4. Try Using a Separate Savings Account: You can monitor your progress towards your goal and prevent using the money for other costs by opening a separate savings account.

Creating sound financial practices will help you in the long run while helping you achieve important milestones. In order to manage your financial destiny, start saving today!

Chapter 5:

Investing for the Long-Term

A key component of accumulating money and gaining financial freedom is long-term investing. While emergency funds and short-term goals can be met with savings, investment can help you reach long-term objectives like retirement or financial freedom. This chapter will discuss the advantages of long-term investing and offer advice on how to manage your investments well.

Some of The Benefits of Long-Term Investing

1. Compound Interest: The power of compound interest is one of the main advantages of long-term investing. Reinvesting your earnings over time might cause your investments to expand exponentially, which can speed up the process of building wealth relative to just saving.

2. Diversification: You can minimize your total risk and diversify your portfolio by investing in a range of assets. You may lessen the effect of market volatility on your portfolio by distributing your investments among a variety of assets, including stocks, bonds, and real estate.

3. Inflation Defense: Over time, investing in assets that outperform inflation can help you maintain your spending power. For instance, buying stocks or real estate can act as a hedge against inflation, which over time can reduce the value of cash.

Tips for Long-Term Investing

1. State Your Goals: Setting goals is crucial before you begin investing. This will enable you to choose the assets you should invest in and your investment plan. For instance, you might want to think about investing in stocks and bonds if you're saving for retirement, while you might want to explore a combination of stocks and cash if you're saving for a down payment on a home.

2. Start Early: Your investments will have more time to compound the earlier you start investing. Even little sums invested consistently over an extended period of time might develop into a sizeable nest egg.

3. Diversify Your Investments: Diversification is essential to lowering your overall risk, as was previously indicated. Put money into a variety of assets that fit your objectives, risk tolerance, and time horizon.

4. Examine Your Tolerance for Risk: Your capacity to take losses on investments depends on your risk tolerance. If market volatility makes you uneasy, you might opt to invest in less risky assets like bonds or cash. However, if you don't mind taking on some risk, you might want to think about buying stocks or real estate.

5. Rebalance Your Portfolio: Your portfolio could go out of balance over time if some assets increase more quickly than others. Your ideal asset allocation can be maintained and your risk can be decreased by periodically rebalancing your portfolio.

6. Invest in Low-Cost Funds: Over time, high fees can reduce your investment returns. Think about investing in low-cost exchange-traded funds (ETFs) or index funds that provide wide market exposure

7. Seek Professional Help: Consider working with a financial advisor if you don't know how to invest or don't have the time to handle your accounts. A competent financial advisor can assist you in creating an investment plan that is specific to your objectives and level of risk tolerance, as well as in managing your investments over time.

8. Don't Time the Market: A dangerous tactic that might result in regrettable financial choices is trying to time the market. Instead, concentrate on creating a diverse portfolio and committing to a long investment horizon.

9. Stay Disciplined: Your discipline may be put to the test as you ride the ups and downs of investing. It's crucial to maintain discipline and refrain from taking snap judgments based on transient market fluctuations. Maintain your investing plan and your long-term objectives in mind.

10. Monitor Your Progress: Finally, it's critical to regularly assess your progress. To stay on track with your objectives, occasionally review your investments and make modifications when necessary. To preserve your target asset allocation, think about rebalancing your portfolio at least once a year.

One of the key components of gaining financial freedom is long-term investing. You may effectively manage your investments and reach your financial goals by taking the time to identify your goals, starting early, diversifying your portfolio, taking your risk tolerance into account, rebalancing your portfolio, and investing in low-cost funds. Keep in mind that investing is a long-term endeavor, so be patient and goal-focused.

Chapter 6:

Understanding Different Types of Investments

There are many various sorts of investment vehicles available when it comes to investing. Every investment kind has a set of distinctive qualities, risks, and potential benefits. Building a portfolio with a diverse range of investments is essential if you want to attain your long-term financial objectives. The most popular investment categories, such as equities, bonds, mutual funds, exchange-traded funds (ETFs), real estate, and alternative investments, will be discussed in this chapter.

1. Stocks: Stocks are ownership stakes in a business that is publicly traded. A stock purchase makes you a shareholder in the firm, giving you the chance to gain from its expansion and success. While stocks may have huge potential profits, they also carry greater dangers. The performance of the firm, market trends, and world events are just a few examples of the many variables that can cause stock prices to be unstable and to change quickly.

2. Bonds: Bonds are debt instruments that have been issued by corporations, governments, and other organizations. In essence, when you purchase a bond, you are making a loan to the issuer and will be paid interest. Bonds have lesser risks than stocks but may have lower potential profits. Bond prices can provide investors with a more stable source of income because they are often less volatile than stock prices.

3. Mutual Funds: Mutual funds are investment vehicles that pool money from many investors to invest in a diversified portfolio of stocks, bonds, or other assets. Mutual funds can offer instant diversification and professional management, making them a popular choice for many investors. However, mutual funds also come with fees and expenses that can eat into your returns.

4. Exchange-Traded Funds (ETFs): ETFs are comparable to mutual funds but trade on stock exchanges like individual stocks. Mutual funds and ETFs both have advantages, such as immediate diversification and expert management, however ETFs may have cheaper costs overall.

5. **Real Estate:** If you want to diversify your investing portfolio, real estate can be a fantastic choice. Rental homes, REITs (real estate investment trusts), and crowdfunding websites are all examples of real estate investments. Real estate can potentially increase in value and provide a source of rental income, but it also has hazards related to upkeep, vacancies, and market volatility.

6. **Alternative Investments:** Investments that don't fall within the usual categories of stocks, bonds, or real estate are referred to as alternative investments. Alternative investments include things like cryptocurrencies, commodities, hedge funds, and private equity. Alternative investments may have a high return potential but also high dangers and a more complex understanding of the investment may be needed.

7. Commodities: Physical products like gold, oil, and crops are considered commodities and can be traded on commodity exchanges. Commodity investing can help you diversify your portfolio, hedge against inflation, and is subject to market and supply and demand swings.

8. Hedge Funds: Hedge funds are financial instruments that employ sophisticated strategies to produce large returns. Hedge funds can have significant fees and expenses and are normally only accessible to accredited investors. Despite the substantial risks they carry and the potential for big rewards, they may not be suited for all investors.

9. Private Equity: Purchasing stock in private companies or contributing to funds that concentrate on them are examples of private equity investments. Investments in private equity may have large potential returns, but they also carry substantial risks and may call for a longer time horizon.

10. Cryptocurrencies: As a new asset class, cryptocurrencies like Bitcoin and Ethereum have grown in popularity in recent years. Although there is a significant possibility for large gains with cryptocurrencies, there are also high hazards involved, including market volatility and regulatory changes.

It's crucial to assess each form of investment in light of your investment objectives, risk tolerance, and time horizon. You can achieve your financial objectives while minimizing risk by creating a well-diversified portfolio that combines a variety of these distinct investment kinds. A financial advisor should always be consulted before making any investing decisions.

Part Three:

Building Wealth and Achieving Financial Freedom

Many people aspire to financial independence and wealth accumulation. However, it can frequently appear to be an impossible endeavor, particularly when dealing with debt, a low salary, or other financial challenges. Fortunately, everyone can accumulate wealth and attain financial freedom with the appropriate mindset, tactics, and practices.

Developing an attitude of abundance and opportunity is one of the first stages in accumulating riches. Focus on what you can do to raise your income and accumulate wealth rather than on shortage or lack. This can entail making a plan, defining goals, and moving through with that plan.

The ability to handle your money well is a crucial component of wealth creation. This entails making a budget, keeping tabs on your spending, and looking for consistent ways to save money.

You can lay a strong financial foundation that will support your long-term wealth creation by lowering your spending and raising your savings.

Investing is yet another crucial element of wealth creation. You may generate passive income, increase your wealth, and achieve financial freedom by making intelligent financial decisions. To reduce risk, you should diversify your portfolio and educate yourself on the various investment kinds, their rewards and risks.

It's crucial to establish sound financial habits and behaviors in addition to managing your money and making intelligent investments. This entails staying out of debt, repaying any debts you do have as soon as you can, and setting up an emergency fund to cover unforeseen costs. It also entails developing disciplined financial habits that you stick to, such setting aside a certain proportion of your income each month or investing on a regular basis.

Last but not least, accumulating wealth and gaining financial freedom involve more than simply money. It also involves clearly defining your life goals and coordinating your money with them. This may entail making decisions and short-term sacrifices in order to accomplish long-term objectives, like starting a business or retiring early.

All things considered, developing wealth and obtaining financial freedom require a combination of attitudes, routines, and tactics. You can achieve financial freedom and enjoy the advantages of wealth for many years by concentrating on increasing your income, properly managing your money, investing intelligently, forming excellent financial habits, and aligning your finances with your life goals.

Chapter 7:

Creating Passive Income Streams

A technique to make money without consistently working for it is through passive income streams. Creating assets that create income on their own, enabling you to make money even while you sleep, is the core of the passive income concept. This chapter will look at various passive income generation strategies that can lead to financial independence.

1. Rental Properties: Being a landlord is a common technique to get passive income. You can make money consistently by renting out a property without actively working for it. Real estate that is rented out might be either residential, commercial, or even a vacation property. Despite the fact that owning rental properties can be a fantastic source of passive income, it necessitates a sizable initial investment and continuing administration.

2. Dividend Stocks: Stocks that regularly distribute a portion of their earnings to owners are known as dividend stocks. You can generate consistent income by purchasing dividend-paying stocks without having to sell your shares. For those looking to invest in the stock market in order to generate passive income, dividend stocks can be a suitable choice.

3. Peer-to-Peer Lending: Platforms for peer-to-peer lending let investors make loans to borrowers directly. You can get consistent interest income from peer-to-peer lending investments without actively managing the loans. Peer-to-peer lending does, however, have hazards, such as platform risks and defaults by borrowers.

4. Creating Digital Products: Digital items like ebooks, courses, and online seminars can be created and sold to generate passive revenue. Once the product is created, you can sell it repeatedly without actively producing new material. A successful digital product, however, needs a lot of work up front and marketing.

5. Affiliate Marketing: Affiliate marketing entails advertising the goods or services of other individuals in exchange for a cut of any purchases generated by your special affiliate link. Affiliate marketing allows you to generate passive revenue by promoting goods that are relevant to your audience on your website or social media accounts.

6. Rental Income from Assets: Renting out property, such as unused equipment, parking spaces, or storage space, can be a way to make passive revenue. You can make a consistent income without actively managing your assets by charging people to utilize them.

Developing passive income streams can help you become financially independent and rely less on active revenue. Before spending your time and money, it's crucial to carefully assess each possibility and weigh the risks and benefits. You can develop a durable source of income that can assist you in reaching your long-term financial objectives by diversifying your passive income streams and concentrating on establishing assets that produce regular and dependable income.

7. Commodities: Physical products like gold, oil, and crops are considered commodities and can be traded on commodity exchanges. Commodity investing can help you diversify your portfolio, hedge against inflation, and is subject to market and supply and demand swings.

8. Hedge Funds: Hedge funds are financial instruments that employ sophisticated techniques to produce large returns. Only accredited investors normally have access to hedge funds, and these investments can have expensive fees and expenditures. Although they carry a high risk and may not be suitable for all investors, they can potentially deliver huge rewards.

9. Private Equity: Purchasing stock in private companies or contributing to funds that concentrate on them are examples of private equity investments. Investments in private equity may have large potential returns, but they also carry substantial risks and may call for a longer time horizon.

10. Cryptocurrencies: As a new asset class, cryptocurrencies like Bitcoin and Ethereum have grown in popularity in recent years. Although there is a significant possibility for large gains with cryptocurrencies, there are also high hazards involved, including market volatility and regulatory changes.

It's crucial to weigh the risks and suitability of various investment kinds for your particular financial condition and goals when you assess various investment options. Additionally, it's crucial to ensure that the fees and costs related to each type of investment are in line with your investment goals by having a comprehensive understanding of them.

In the end, a well-diversified portfolio with a variety of investments can assist you in achieving your long-term financial objectives while minimizing risk. Before making any investment decisions, always do your homework and speak with a financial expert to be sure you are acting responsibly and sensibly with your money.

Chapter 8:

Real Estate Investing

One of the most well-liked strategies for accumulating wealth and achieving financial independence is real estate investing. In addition to having the potential for long-term appreciation and wealth creation, it can offer a consistent flow of passive income. But it's critical to approach real estate investing with a thorough awareness of the dangers and benefits, as well as the different approaches and methods involved.

Learning about the various property kinds, financing alternatives, and investment methods is one of the first steps to successful real estate investing. This could entail reading books, going to seminars, or talking to a real estate expert. You can choose which techniques and properties to pursue by having a basic understanding of real estate investing.

Rental property investing is one of the most popular real estate investment ideas. Buying a property and renting it to tenants, usually for a monthly fee, is what this entails. Investments in rental properties have the potential to generate a consistent stream of passive income as well as long-term growth and wealth creation. The property must be kept up, repairs must be made as needed, and tenants must be thoroughly vetted.

Flipping homes is another kind of real estate investing. This entails getting a house, fixing it up, and then offering it for sale. Although flipping houses can be a profitable strategy, it comes with a lot of risk and takes a lot of time, money, and effort to execute well.

Other real estate investment techniques to take into account include purchasing commercial real estate, investing in real estate investment trusts (REITs), and taking part in real estate crowdfunding platforms. These tactics are in addition to buying rental properties and flipping homes.

There are several choices to think about when it comes to financing real estate transactions. Traditional mortgages, private lenders, hard money loans, and even crowdfunding may fall under this category. Every financing option has advantages and disadvantages, so it's crucial to thoroughly weigh your alternatives before selecting the one that best suits your financial status and investment goal.

Understanding the local market and being current on trends and developments are also crucial for real estate investment success. Researching vacancy rates, rental costs, and property values in various neighborhoods, as well as keeping an eye on regional economic conditions and development plans, may be required for this. You can choose which properties to invest in and when to buy or sell by remaining knowledgeable about the local market.

Property management is a key component of real estate investing. You will be responsible for managing tenant issues, repairs, and maintenance if you intend to rent out your properties. The upkeep of a successful real estate portfolio may be a time-consuming and occasionally difficult undertaking. You could choose to outsource these duties to a property management business, but doing so would increase your costs and decrease your revenue.

Finally, when it comes to real estate investing, it's critical to adopt a long-term perspective. Even though there may be opportunities to earn quick money by flipping or renting out properties for a short period of time, the most prosperous real estate investors concentrate on developing a long-term portfolio of lucrative properties that may offer consistent passive income and increase in value over time. You may attain financial independence and create lasting wealth through the power of real estate by adopting a patient and strategic approach to investing in real estate.

Chapter 9:

Starting and Growing a Business

Building wealth and achieving financial freedom can be done very effectively by starting and growing a successful business. To improve your chances of success, it's crucial to approach entrepreneurship with rigorous planning and preparation.

The essential processes for beginning and expanding a business will be covered in this chapter, including:

1. Identifying a market need and developing a business idea
2. Conducting market research and developing a business plan
3. Securing funding and resources
4. Launching and growing your business
5. Managing and scaling your business over time

1. Identifying a market need and developing a business idea

Finding a market need or gap that your firm can fill is the first step in launching a successful venture. This might entail looking at market trends and client demands, as well as seeing any weaknesses that competitors might have.

It's crucial to create a business idea that creatively and persuasively answers a possible market need after you've discovered it. This can entail coming up with brand-new goods or services, improving current ones, or creating a fresh corporate strategy or model.

2. Conducting market research and developing a business plan

The next stage after having a distinct business concept is to carry out market research and create a thorough business plan. This may entail studying your target market, examining market trends and rivals, and creating a precise marketing, sales, and operations strategy.

A solid business plan should outline your products or services in great depth, analyze your target market, break down your initial expenses and financial requirements, and lay out a clear plan for generating income and attaining long-term growth.

3. Securing funding and resources

The next stage after having a well-defined business plan is to obtain the capital and resources required to start and expand your company. This may entail receiving a loan from a bank or other financial institution, securing investment from venture capitalists or angel investors, or bootstrapping your business using personal resources or credit.

Along with money, it's crucial to put together a team of bright and motivated people who can assist you in starting and expanding your firm. In order to gain access to vital resources and knowledge, this may entail recruiting staff, making contracts with independent contractors or consultants, or collaborating with other companies or organizations.

4. Launching and growing your business

It's time to launch and expand your firm once you've gotten the money and resources you need. This might involve creating a solid web presence, doing a good job of marketing your goods or services, and cultivating enduring connections with clients and business partners.

It's critical to maintain flexibility as your company expands and makes adjustments to meet shifting customer demands and market conditions. To achieve this, you might need to change your business strategy, enter new markets or product categories, or create new alliances or collaborations.

5. Managing and scaling your business over time

As your company grows, it's crucial to concentrate on controlling and expanding your operations to boost productivity and profitability. This could entail putting in place new systems and procedures to optimize operations, cultivating trusted relationships with suppliers and vendors, and making investments in cutting-edge machinery or technology to boost output and quality.

Ultimately, staying devoted, adaptable, and focused on your long-term objectives is the key to success in beginning and expanding a business. You can create a successful and long-lasting business that can assist you in achieving financial independence and long-term prosperity by remaining aware of market trends and client needs, cultivating good relationships with stakeholders, and consistently upgrading your operations and services.

Part Four:

Maintaining Financial Success

The importance of maintaining financial success cannot be overstated. In order to maintain your success once you have established a solid financial foundation and made good investments, it is crucial to maintain effective money management.

Reviewing and modifying your financial plan on a frequent basis is essential for maintaining financial success. This entails regularly reviewing your goals, investments, and budget and making any required adjustments to make sure you are still on pace to reach them.

Avoiding pointless risks is a crucial component of maintaining financial success. This entails exercising caution when making investments, staying away from risky ones that could result in large losses, and diversifying your portfolio to minimize your exposure to risk.

It's also critical to keep learning about investment and personal finance. To keep up with the newest trends and methods for wise money management, attend seminars, read books, and speak with financial experts.

In addition to doing these actions, it's critical to maintain discipline and prevent developing poor money habits. Living within your means, avoiding pointless debt, and striking a healthy balance between spending and saving are all important in order to achieve this.

In the end, continuing effort and commitment are necessary to maintain financial success. You can achieve long-term financial stability and security by focusing on your goals and making wise financial decisions.

Chapter 10:

Protecting Your Wealth with Insurance

A crucial instrument for safeguarding your wealth and maintaining financial security is insurance. We will discuss the many types of insurance that are offered in this chapter, as well as how they may be used to protect your assets and reduce risks.

Insurance Forms

There are numerous kind of insurance available, each one intended to guard against a particular danger. The following are a few of the most popular types of insurance:

1. Health insurance - Protects you against the price of medical costs, such as physician visits, hospital stays, and prescription medications.

2. Life insurance - Offers your loved ones financial support in the case of your passing.

3. Disability insurance - If you become disabled and are unable to work, this insurance replaces your income.

4. Auto insurance - Guards you against monetary losses brought on by mishaps or car theft.

5. Homeowners insurance - Covers loss or damage from fire, theft, or other covered events to your house and personal property.

6. Umbrella Insurance - Offers extra liability protection on top of your current plans.

Benefits of Insurance

Insurance provides many benefits, including:

1. Risk Mitigation - Insurance lessens the financial toll that unplanned occurrences like illness, accidents, or natural disasters might have.

2. Peace of Mind - Feeling secure in the knowledge that you are safeguarded from unforeseeable catastrophes might come from having insurance coverage.

3. Financial security - Insurance can act as a safety net in times of need, ensuring that you have the resources necessary to pay for unforeseen costs.

4. Asset Protection - Insurance works to shield your possessions from theft or damage, allowing you to accumulate and safeguard your money over time.

Choosing the Right Insurance

It's crucial to thoroughly assess your needs and choose the appropriate type and level of coverage when purchasing insurance. Considerable factors include:

1. Your risk profile - Take into account the dangers you are most likely to encounter and choose insurance that will adequately protect you from them.

2. Your Budget - Take into account the price of insurance premiums and choose coverage that is in line with your spending limit.

3. Policy Features - Look for policies with features that meet your specific needs, such as deductible amounts, coverage limits, and add-on options.

4. Company Reputation - Choose insurance providers with a strong reputation for quality service and financial stability.

In addition to selecting the right insurance coverage, there are also steps you can take to maximize the benefits of your insurance policies. These include:

1. Understanding Your Policy - Read and comprehend your insurance policy, including the exclusions, deductibles, and coverage limits. This will help you prevent unpleasant surprises and make sure you have complete coverage in case of need.

2. Regularly reviewing your coverage - As your situation changes, it's possible that your insurance requirements would as well. Make careful to examine your coverage frequently and alter your policy as necessary.

3. Keeping Good Records - Keep accurate records of your insurance plans, including policy numbers, coverage thresholds, and insurer contact information. This will make filing claims simpler and guarantee that you have the coverage you require.

4. Consulting a Reliable expert - To assist you in making an informed insurance decision and navigating the market, think about consulting a reliable financial expert or insurance agent.

You may optimize the advantages of your plans and secure long-term financial security by following these steps and adopting a proactive approach to managing your insurance coverage.

In conclusion, insurance is a vital tool for safeguarding your assets and reducing risk. You can obtain financial stability and peace of mind by being aware of the various forms of insurance that are available, choosing the appropriate coverage, and taking action to maximize the advantages of your plans.

Chapter 11:

Estate Planning and Legacy Building

In the case of your death or incapacitation, managing and dispersing your assets is the process of estate planning. It is a crucial component of financial planning because it guarantees that your loved ones will be taken care of and that your assets will be allocated in accordance with your intentions. Planning for end-of-life care and minimizing taxes and fees related with asset transfers are also part of estate planning.

On the other side, legacy building entails identifying your beliefs, objectives, and future vision and utilizing your assets and resources to realize them. It is about leaving a meaningful legacy that represents your values and objectives and making a long-lasting impression.

Here are some important components of estate planning and legacy building:

1. Making a Will - A will is a legal document that specifies how your possessions should be dispersed in the event of your passing. It may also contain guidelines for planning a funeral and looking after young children.

2. Creating Trusts - Trusts are legal agreements that let you give control of your assets to a trustee for management and distribution in accordance with your wishes. Taxes can be reduced, probate can be avoided, and beneficiaries with little children or disabilities can be taken care of thanks to trusts.

3. Designating Beneficiaries - Make sure to designate beneficiaries for your life insurance policies, retirement accounts, and other assets that support beneficiary designations. Through the avoidance of probate, this makes sure that these assets are allocated in accordance with your intentions.

4. Planning for End-of-Life Care - To guarantee that your wishes for end-of-life care are respected, think about drafting a living will or healthcare proxy. This may entail appointing a power of attorney to handle your medical affairs.

5. **Charitable Giving** - If you want to leave a lasting legacy and support causes that are important to you, think about incorporating charitable giving into your estate plan.

6. **Reviewing and Changing Your Plan** - Make sure to frequently evaluate and change your estate plan to make sure it still reflects your current goals and situation.

Creating a goal for your life and using your resources to realize it are both components of legacy building. It could entail donating to charities, setting up a family foundation, or starting a scholarship fund. It's about making a difference and leaving a lasting legacy.

In conclusion, legacy creation and estate planning are crucial aspects of financial planning. In addition to ensuring that your assets are dispersed in accordance with your preferences, they also reduce taxes and other costs while also financing end-of-life care. Creating a goal for your life and using your resources to realize it are both components of legacy building. You can make sure that your loved ones are taken care of and that your legacy represents your values and objectives by taking a proactive approach to estate planning and legacy building.

Chapter 12:

Staying on Track and Adjusting Your Strategy

Congratulations! You have developed a solid financial foundation, created passive income streams, set up savings and investment programs, and secured your money through estate planning and insurance. You are already a long way from being financially free. The journey does not, however, finish here. Staying on course and making necessary plan adjustments are crucial for maintaining your financial success.

1. Maintaining Focus

Maintaining your financial plan and tracking your success are key to staying on track. Regularly assessing your spending and budget is one method to do this. This will enable you to spot potential areas of overspending and make necessary modifications to stay inside your financial goal. Additionally, it is crucial to often check on your investments to make sure they are working as anticipated.

2. Modifying Your Approach

Your financial objectives and priorities may change as your living circumstances do. For instance, if you have children, you might want to change your savings strategy to account for college costs. In order to reduce risk and guarantee a regular income stream as you approach retirement, you might need to modify your investment strategy. To make sure that your financial plan is still applicable and useful, it is crucial to periodically review it and make any necessary revisions.

3. consulting a financial advisor

Having a financial counselor by your side might be a great way to keep on track and modify your plan. A financial advisor can offer advice on making investments, assist you in understanding complex tax rules, and give you useful market trend analysis. A financial counselor can also assist you in developing a long-term financial strategy that takes into consideration your particular objectives and situation.

4. Upholding Good Financial Practices

Finally, keeping on track and succeeding financially depends on upholding sound financial practices. This involves maintaining a regular savings and investment schedule, managing your debt, and living within your means. You can make sure that your financial plan continues to work as intended and that you keep moving in the right direction by establishing and upholding sound financial practices.

Here are some extra suggestions that you should take into account;

1. Measuring Progress: It's critical to regularly evaluate your financial progress to see if you're on track to reach your objectives. This may entail checking the success of your investments, keeping tabs on your earnings and expenses, and assessing your debt loads.

2. Overcoming Setbacks: On your road to financial success, you may encounter stumbling blocks like unforeseen bills or job loss. It's crucial to have a strategy in place for how to handle these circumstances and keep moving forward with your objectives.

3. Motivation: It takes discipline and persistence to accumulate and preserve riches. To assist keep you motivated and on track, it can be beneficial to create a support structure, such as a financial accountability partner.

4. Giving Back: After achieving financial success, supporting worthwhile causes or giving back to your community can be satisfying. This may entail giving to charities, doing volunteer work, or engaging in other acts of philanthropy. These values can provide your financial journey a feeling of direction and fulfillment if you include them into your financial strategy.

5. Tax planning: Your tax obligations change as your financial condition does. Maintaining financial success requires careful tax preparation because it can reduce tax liabilities and increase profits. Knowing your tax bracket, the various credits and deductions, and incorporating tax-efficient investing methods into your overall financial strategy are all necessary for this.

6. Managing Risk: There is always a certain amount of risk associated with making an investment. To safeguard your wealth, it's critical to assess and manage risk effectively. This may entail diversifying your investment holdings, getting insurance, and staying away from high-risk bets.

7. It can be difficult to strike a balance between your immediate requirements and your long-term financial objectives. It's critical to have a strategy in place for handling unforeseen costs while continuing to save money for the future. This may entail setting up an emergency fund, choosing achievable goals, and exercising financial restraint.

8. Maintaining a Healthy Credit Score: Access to credit and favorable interest rates are dependent on having a high credit score. By keeping your debt to a minimum, paying your payments on time, and keeping an eye on your credit report, you may maintain a decent credit score.

9. Lifestyle Inflation: It may be alluring to up your spending when your income rises. But this could result in lifestyle inflation, when your costs increase in line with your income. It's critical to control lifestyle inflation and keep a balanced ratio of spending to saving.

20. Last but not least, it's critical to frequently review your financial goals and make any necessary adjustments to your strategy. Making adjustments to your investing strategy or savings plan may be one way to do this, along with reevaluating your priorities and your progress.

You may contribute to maintaining financial success over the long run by addressing these issues and putting them into your financial plan. You may attain financial freedom and create a secure future for yourself and your loved ones with discipline, planning, and a commitment to your goals.

CONCLUSION

Although understanding your finances is not simple, the effort is unquestionably worthwhile. Financial freedom requires time, perseverance, discipline, and—most importantly—a readiness to change and grow.

We have looked at the fundamentals of money management throughout this book, from creating a solid financial foundation to generating passive income streams, from real estate investing to launching and growing a business, from using insurance to protect your wealth to estate planning and legacy building.

You can take charge of your finances, accumulate wealth, and attain financial freedom by putting the concepts and tactics described in this book into practice. You will gain the confidence necessary to make wise choices, establish and meet your financial objectives, and build the life of your dreams.

Keep in mind that achieving financial freedom does not require being wealthy or possessing large sums of cash. It is about being able to enjoy life on your terms, unburdened by the stress and concerns of a precarious financial situation. It is all about enjoying the security and peace of mind that come from knowing that you are in charge of your financial situation and future.

Therefore, start today by mastering your finances. Start putting the concepts and tactics described in this book into practice, and watch as your financial situation changes right before your eyes. You can discover the keys to financial freedom and lead the life of your dreams if you put in the effort, work hard, and make a commitment to lifelong learning.

www.ingramcontent.com/pod-product-compliance
Lightning Source LLC
Chambersburg PA
CBHW070435220526
45466CB00004B/1687